the holy ground

the holy ground

michael carey

12/5/03

Michael Carey
Orange City.

carrauntoohil books
farragut, iowa
2003

For Keith e
Marabel
Thank you again
for opening your
home e hearts
To this wayfaring
stranger.
May the holy ground
you stand on always
hold firm e maintain.

ISBN   0-9725606-0-2 paper

Photograph of Michael Carey copyright by Owen Carey Studios, Portland, Oregon
Cover art, pastel drawing, "The Carey Home Place," copyright 2002 by Bobbie McKibbin, Grinnell, Iowa
Printing by Sheridan Books, Ann Arbor, Michigan

Publisher's Address

Carrauntoohil Books
PO Box 18
1980 380th Avenue
Farragut, Iowa 51639
(712) 246-3453 (fax & ph)
loesshillsbks@heartland.net

also by michael carey

poetry
The Noise the Earth Makes
Honest Effort
Nishnabotna
Carpenter of Song
Voices on the Landscape (editor)

plays
A Song in the Wilderness
Dear Iowa (co-author)

teaching manual
Poetry: Starting from Scratch

for Kelly
and the soil that sustains us

contents

1 -- the holy ground

II –– out of the body travel

III –– a place at the table

acknowledgements

biography

1

the holy ground

the arrogance of staying put

What do you think
when you drive by
on Route 80
with your eyes
listening for
the faint call
of the distant mountains,
that everything around
is empty and flat and boring?
Admit it, you've
used those words
when you could
have said "green,"
when you could have said
"beautiful" or "vast"
or "balanced."
Admit that you
don't know where
you're driving
or what you're
driving over.
How could you?
Who does?
That when you
arrive where
you intend,
someone is
always there
before you
asking for money.
Listen, and
I mean listen,
stop if you
have to, where-
ever you are,
whoever you are,
whatever you left,

wherever you are going,
everything that matters
is here. It's here. Right here
and it always has been.

the holy ground

for Gilbert and Liz Barraza

In a church in Juarez, before I journeyed from El Paso to Las Cruces and Albuquerque then on to Santa Fe, two friends, locals, insisted that I go to Chimayo. "There's a church there" she said, "with a hole in it you can reach down into and pick up handfuls of dirt to rub on your hurting body. Many have been helped and healed." He tried to make a yearly pilgrimage. She wanted to bring their baby there as soon as it was born. "The churchyard," she said "was littered with discarded wheelchairs and walkers and canes" -- the refuse of Heaven's miraculous power.

Unfortunately, snow, the interests of fellow-travelers and the miles we had to go kept me from visiting. But I know what I would have found. I have already found it. Even now, at home in Iowa, I am holding it in my hands. A ground so holy that, every so many years, I am born again from it, actually, not metaphorically: a new heart, a new brain, new skin, new liver -- everything -- as I imagine it was or should be. Again and again, day after day, year after year, molecule by molecule, the old worn-out parts of my former self fall away like once-beautiful clothes that I have now outgrown, and I am made over. At least one atom in my body, in every body, I have read, was once in the body of Christ. No need to ask for new legs; I already have them. No need to ask for new arms and hands; they are already holding the soil that holds me, that dirties them. See how they smudge the air till the land glitters in dust where my name is written, where all names are written before they dissipate and fall like a dark rain, like prayers said in silence, like certain sweet songs of longing we all sing, constantly, only God can hear.

setting traps

As a boy, he found he was good with his hands. He made things with them. He could twist wire into designs from which no animal could escape. So, he set traps: by the creek, in the fields, on the hillsides. All creation, he killed and kept for his own. But, unless he was hungry, he could not enjoy so many lifeless things. So, he trapped animals live and watched them and listened to them: little mice, badgers, raccoon, mink, beaver -- anything and everything that came to him. In the end, they died anyway. Despite his efforts, all creation seemed sullen, determined to keep its secrets.

What he really wanted was what he could not catch, what could not *be* caught. But he could only do what he was good at. So he went on building traps: bigger, stronger, each one more complex and subtle. He no longer used metal. Sometimes he used straw or sticks, sometimes words or touch or prayer. His plans became so elaborate, even he forgot how they were laid and where or how deep. In the end, as you might expect, he was caught in a trap of his own devising, a trap so pure and so light, he did not mind. He could hardly tell when he was caught or free. He could just feel, at times, something he did not understand, something himself and something other, something simple and something clever, something he could no longer control or describe, every once in a while, taking hold and, slowly, drawing him in.

on constancy and change

how we felt the first flush of fresh air
once we opened the sash
in summer's hot and fusty bedroom

* * * * * * * * * * * * * * *

how clear the bath seemed
after years of washing in well water,
our baked bodies red from the gifts
the earth so extravagantly offered

* * * * * * * * * * * * * * *

how the air that
touched the ground
touched our crops
touched our tractors
touched us,
before we
built cabs
and shut the doors
and turned on
the conditioner

* * * * * * * * * * * * * * * *

one hundred and seventeen all July
all January, fifty below
and God knows what
with the wind-chill factored

what relief,
what joy,
the change of seasons,
the God-awful hurt
and the spirit's sudden mending

* * * * * * * * * * * * * * * *

the earth still turns
the leaves still fall
and snow still hushes every worry
just bend back your head and look;
the sun and the moon assure you:
it is not they who have changed

once when the ground was holy

for Jon Chenette

I

Once when the
ground was holy,
you could enter it
and come out again;
the dust that
covered your dust
did no harm;
the light that
entered your bones
when all went dark
sent you out again
with dew, with dew
on the tips of your wings.

II

Once when the
ground was holy,
we'd rise
when earth's red eye
came for us.
We'd work and work,
like it or not,
till the end
of the day
when we'd fall
refreshed,
where the night
stood waiting
and the trees
and the silence
in their branches;

waiting, waiting,
all waiting
patiently
as always
for something
that was
not us.

III

Once when the
ground was holy,
horses, more horses
than you could believe,
would walk
through leaves
and make
no sound.
In autumn
you would
find them
in the pasture
or on the wild hillside
where they played
and grazed
drinking deeply
from some
strange water.
Sometimes, when
the weather
was right,
they would
let you ride them
if you wished,
if you wished,
if you
remembered how.

IV

Once when the
ground was holy,
there was no difference
between what was said
and what was done,
between the metaphor
and the life.
When one "went to the well,"
one went to the well
and often.
When one dropped a rope
in the darkness,
the darkness echoed
and sustained
because there was
a real wooden bucket
at the end of it.

V

Once when the
ground was holy
people did not
look for what they
could not find;
what they
could not find
found them.
They did not
ask if God
was dead,
they heard Him,
heard It, Her,
they heard
what they
were born

to become
rolling like
thunder
inside them.

VI

Once when the
ground was holy,
the sounds
one made
reached other ears,
when there was
work to be done,
there were other
hands to help,
bodies were born
and born again,
they ate and lived
and knew it.
They felt it, heard it
in the space
between their bones.
Silence
had not spread
its ignorant hand
over green fields,
over yellow,
over vast and fertile pockets,
its dark, joyless hand
groping, always groping
for money.

VII

Once when the
ground was holy

men did not
rip it and
feed it poison
and flush it
downstream
to forgotten
depths of
faraway water.
Like the lilies
of the field
it fed them,
when it had
a mind to,
when those
that lived
on it
asked little
and got much,
when they took
what they
were given
and said
thank you,
when they
had a mind to.
After they ate
they sat still
and listened.
The dreams
of the world
rising all
around them.

VIII

Once when the
ground was holy,
people left --

butcher, baker, beggar man, thief,
saint, sinner, scholar --
wherever they were,
whatever they were doing,
when ice melted,
when brown turned green,
when wind came and came
and blew the souls
right out of them,
when each blade of grass
danced naked
at its own resurrection.

fences

There aren't that many
pigs or cattle or chickens
on the farm anymore.
We save most of the animals now
for the big boys,
in the slick-tied corporations.
So the fences have come down
and the fields grown together
and the eye accustomed
to a vaster landscape.
But, sometimes I need a wall or two
to know who I am,
that I am, something here
or there that won't move,
some other's skin to touch,
a different pair of eyes to look
up at me with unknowing
unfathomable wonder and trust.
Over the years,
these are the cries that
have kept me tied to home.
These are the anchors
that have kept my soul
from drifting. That gave rise,
in the first place, to the idea of escape.

WORMS

They really know how
to get to the bottom of things.
Their work is their life.
They have no dwelling.
These tillers of the soil,
these lovers of the earth
who caress the ground
the entire length of their bodies,
their whole lives long.
Who else can say he never left it,
that he kisses it daily,
sleeps with it, in it,
eats it morning
noon and night,
that he excretes it,
that he helps it breathe,
letting the food it needs
be served in the space
he leaves behind.

Slowly, with dignity, they inch
their selves through the world
excruciatingly on the way
to nowhere, to the dirt,
to right where they started.
And for all their struggle,
who admires them? Who loves them
but birds and fishermen,
and children
who squish them between their fingers,
who step on them and cry,
when, after a rain, they rise
by the thousands,
gasping for darkness,
drowning in the open air?

once by the flooded creek

Once by the muddy
flooded creek,
I stood
staring at the damage
the beavers had done
when the brown bank
moved in the shape
of a large turtle.
He didn't seem to care
that I was there.
It was almost as if
I didn't matter.
He chewed for awhile
on something green,
an hour, or two,
maybe three -- who knows
how long between bites
he lay thinking
about what is
before he disappeared
back into the slime
he rose from?

shit

for Denise and Bill Ryan

The dog comes
bounding toward you
smelling of it,
the dust of the barnyard
clinging like gray moss
on his white fur.
He is happy.
He licks your hand
and does not care
that you have your own
queer fragrance.
Your boots, too, tell
many dirty little stories
about cow shit,
pig shit, chicken shit,
horse shit, cat shit, bull shit,
crap, excrement, manure,
muffins and pies... .
How many days have you
stood in it and shoveled it,
taken it, flung it, given it,
pumped it and spread
its iridescent honey
over the fields
to make them clean again,
green again and new,
once the warm winds come
and the cold wet winter
is over?

WATER

It bows constantly before
the great god
gravity. It was born
with no will
of its own, and
never attained one.
It follows the orders
of whatever
stands in its way.
Even the far off tiny sun
sets it running
in circles.
A pale issue of the marriage
between hydrogen and oxygen,
everyone's empty-headed friend
calmly drying in your hands
becoming in time:
a sigh, sweat, release,
the giant storm
that is always coming,
that is prayed for even
in the withering fields.

fire

Two days after I lit them,
the tower of twigs
finally catch.
Unexpected winds
blow the smallest embers
into the largest conflagration --
a creek-mile of elms,
and locust and cottonwood
pushed into a pile
surrounded by weeds,
even overgrown by them,
and volunteer grasses and vines.

One day the dozer will return
and scrape a hole to swallow
what blackened rumps
of evidence remain.
The astonished beaver,
who have already ruined
so much good ground,
dampened and suffocated
so many roots and sustaining tendrils,
look out on a brightness
even their small brains know enough
to hide from.
I started it and I didn't.
It calls out loudly
in a primitive tongue,
words that do not comfort.

horizon

Don't call it
a bunch of dirt.

Don't call it
water.

Don't say it's grass
waving in the wind.

Don't say there
are people on it,

distant trees
with their roots

in the sky and their
creaking branches

trying to balance
what is rolling.

It's more than that,
surely. It's more.

In any country,
on every continent,

in the eye
of every beholder,

come evening,
from every direction,

birds pull
the shadow

of God's hand
over it.

sleepwalking

At night, when you
turn out the light,
you disappear; your being
from your body disengages.
It is what floats over
the bed and stares down
at what, just a moment ago,
was you. It is what
the dogs sense out over
the corn and in the mist
on the lowland by the creek –
it is why they are barking.
They aren't trying to protect
your home and your family
and your belongings;
they're letting you know
where, exactly, home is.
They're reminding you that
they have bodies too
and that they live in them
energetically, contentedly,
all their short lives
as long as you are there
to look into their animal eyes
and speak to them softly
and rub your calloused hands
over their muddy fur.
Before you get too far,
listen to their rough voices
calling you back to the
unplanted seed you left again,
so carelessly, lying down
in the dark dirt of the farm.

Fishing

Here I am again
on the edge of the pond,
baiting the hook
with whatever I can find
in the muffled grasses.
I look into the dark water
and see nothing
although at night
I can hear the
silver tails splashing.
In the morning
I find beavers have
dammed something else.
Here a ripple — there
a ripple — something
beyond thought moving
just below the surface.

Everyday I come here
although I haven't
the faintest idea
what I am doing.
The confusion, the
hook bites on my fingers,
the clouds swirling
mysteriously above me
are all a part
of the joyous plan.

Someday I know the line
will bump and tighten,
something bright will
begin thrashing,
some unknown trembling
will pull at my fingers
and, whether I throw
it back or not,

the white meat
I catch will feed
the hunger inside me.

legacy

After a storm, words
fell upon the earth,

too heavy to be lifted,
too light to lie down,

too fluid to stick
upon a surface.

Often, I have felt particles
passing through me

on their way to some place
indescribable without them,

passing on to you,
if *you* is the right term

for the individual spirit
inside the individual brain,

behind the blinking eyes letting
these dark fragments of light in –

these echoes of the
unpronounceable

lying about the dark forest of the world
like so much dead wood.

Leslie's Grave

Winter

I

Fall into snow,
and the body's
warm flesh
makes a hole
deep and straight
for a moment
and steaming.

II

The wreath
we left
last Christmas
fell into
a tall drift.
It tilted and fell
when winter came.
It is falling still
because there is
nowhere
for the wind
to take it.

III

On each stone,
a name
by each name,
a date and
a few well-
chosen words –

and a cold white hush
over all of them.

IV

What is winter for
but leaving:
your mother,
your father,
your grandparents
before them,
your aunt and uncle,
and now a lovely
lively sister, oh,
that you have to
freeze your fingers
to find?

V

In a field
of crosses
on the open earth
hang a hundred
broken Christs,
and on every
granite wound,
over every punctured heart,
all one can see
are icicles.

Spring

I

It is coming

though we still
can't believe it.
Brown blemishes
on the maple's arm.

II

A few broken sticks,
a few scattered leaves,
one or two footprints
in the hardened mud.
All that's left
of autumn's sorrow.

III

Everywhere,
snow's white blanket
threadbare and dirty.
Was that an insect I
heard, just now, singing?
It couldn't have been,
but I know I heard it.

IV

In the cold rain
every bowed head
is bent
toward the recalcitrant sun.

V

Underground
something is stirring,

something dark,
something white,
some ageless rumor of green.

It is quiet--
shh! Only
if you kneel
and put your ear
to the ground,
will you hear it.

Summer

I

Last week
the wind blew down
the old cedar
and the termites
in its broken branches
still have not noticed.
The full length of it,
they are digging.

II

There are so many paths
through the deep grass.
They all lead
to your bronze face
blooming in the soil.

III

It is morning
and the stars

are shining.
The moon continues
to beckon overhead
pointing the way home.

IV

Whoever it was
who passed by
searching for something
is gone now
into the green
distance.

V

An owl hoots
in the elms.
I try not to listen.
I go about my business.
Quietly, I go about my business
so it will
go on singing.

Autumn

Here, here,
still here
on the green hill
undulating
above the trace,
under the rusty arms
of the giant cedar.

Something keeps me
coming back, something,

back to your tomb
and the wind making
the insides flutter.

Something
fills the space
between my body
and the ground,
between your face
and our final
resting place.

O, Heaven is here,
it's here, sister,
where the limp leaves
are falling.

shear wind

Nothing can keep
the barn up now.
The coop, its
rusty nails
and weathered boards,
are past holding.

For the last
twenty years
you've shouldered
the doors and the beams
so the pickup and the tractor
could pass through
and you could
stack the past
into neat piles
for the future.

Now the eaves
are lifting
and you
can see stars
pouring through
the life you built
and attempted to save.

Oh, there
will be
a great silence
when the wind
stops blowing,
an infinite absence
of sound. Keep
the animals warm.
Talk to them.
Dry them. Tell them
you don't know what

is happening. The whole
sparkling and expectant world
will want to know
what you do then.

the wind in the wires

I walk alone as evening falls
on the gravel road,
not even the dog
by my side,
just the threat
of rain hovering,
and this nonexistent ocean,
an ear to the shell of the world,
a train I never did see coming,
a whole squadron of invisible planes,
a ghost of myself,
tapping me on the back,
making the brittle grasses creak,
a moan, a howl, an eagle, a hawk,
a sudden shudder in my clothes
haunting me all the way
out to the blacktop.

jackstraw

There are farmers in these parts
who could count on their two hands
and their two feet if need be,
all the words they have spoken
in their long lives.

It is as if their time on earth
was inversely proportional
to the number of syllables
they let pass through their lips.

What use are whole mountains of language
when everyone knows
what the problem is,
when everyone knows
what you mean,
what you want,
what you need;
when every night after the day's labors
you and you neighbors
lie down in the dark dirt
unspeakably endless?

Lowland

It is where water goes
when it is tired of going.
It is the sky on the ground
between your toes.
It is where everything
you sent out
comes flooding back,
like you knew it would,
on its slow journey home.

for kelly

After the day's labor
my sun-shrunken body
spirals into bed.
Grief, old and familiar,
wells in my lungs,
so I bury my face
in your hair
and breathe in
the fresh air
you have saved
for me. Gently
my hand traces
the curve
of your back,
its soft skin
rising and falling
in darkness.

Almost hovering,
my fingers dip
into the hard hollow
by your hips and climb
up again, out again
onto more tender country.
Oh then, only then,
do I find what I am
searching for and allow
a dream to take me.

the mirror

The sands in this glass
have been falling
for over 100 years.
You'd think by now
they would have stopped
in a puddle on the floor.
But no, they keep falling.
Face after face after face
in my family have looked in it
and seen their lives,
more or less, revealed.
It's a wonder the washcloth
doesn't set my darkened skin to rippling.
Still, each morning
I start the day
staring at the face on the face
of our forebears,
riding the breaking waves
downward.

for the twenty-fifth anniversary of your death

for Helen Singler Carey

I never thought I'd live past
the age you were when you died
or that I should. Now,
in a few short years
that day will arrive.

The promise
I whispered,
so long ago,
I still remember.

Mother, it's not my heart anymore,
but my body and my bones
that are breaking.

I just wanted to tell you.
I just wanted you to know,
I have never seen a Fall
more beautiful.

Fungi

The rain brings
you out, the
cool damp air,
the dark night
that passes. He who
thinks nothing immense
secretly happens in
the suddenly barren soil,
should find a tree
or a rotten twig
and look closely
at the ground.
Without moving
or making a sound,
immeasurable hosts gather.
White shrouds rise
as strong woody meat
falls down,
falls down and dissolves.

farm angel

Who knows what implement
stirs the black earth beside us?
Our green lives reach out,
rooted, silent and unseen.
Footsteps pass, then the
sound of careful chopping.
We think we know
who the arms belong to,
whose ubiquitous step
leaves its faint
footprint in the dark.

mud

Okay, it *is* gross,
but it is welcome -- slippery
sloppy, dirty, clinging.
It sucks.
Every spring
the pubic mound
of nature becomes
excited again,
lubricated,
awaiting the seed
of whatever is planted.
Husbandman,
this is a sacred, timeless act
you are performing
for the betterment
or the detriment
of the human family.
You had better be in love.
This is not *business*.
You are in a bed
about to burst
into blossom.

wings

Over the farm
the eagle hovers, the hawk,
an owl, a vulture
circling, watching.
One by one,
they ruffle their feathers
and fall through
a clarity they
could never understand,
never even see.
An emptiness
holds them fixed
to the heavens
until they find
what they are
looking for and dive:
a snake,
a mouse,
a chicken,
a wounded raccoon
by the creek,
a dead dog
on the road
with cars
full of humans
endlessly passing.

spade work

Who is your poem for
oh tree, oh rock;
for whom does
the creek glisten?
For millions of years
they have sung their song and died.
What ancient tunes
now rest in my hands,
these rude and unworthy hands
that never tire of digging?

cockfight

There is no betting
at this one,
no crowds,
just hens
in the yard
under elms
and maples.

Up in the air
they scream and leap,
the horrendous spurs
at the back of their legs
and their sharp bloody talons
pummeling, scratching feathers
and the tender meat below,
and picking at each other's eyes.
What do the ladies
make of these warriors
fighting for their favor?
They have peace
and quiet for a while.
They cluck
about whatever
their small brains
think is worthy:
pebbles and stones
and worms, I suppose.

When I first started
farming I was told,
"There should be nine hens
for every one rooster,
nine or you will turn
your fine-feathered females
into prostitutes,
they will become
haggard, bald and battered

while the roosters
go after each other
until they die.
One rooster for
every nine hens
and they'll all stay
healthy and fine."

You can set
the numbers correctly,
but a hen here or there
might die or go exploring
and never come home,
meet up with a fox or a
low-flying owl in the evening.
Lord knows, there are plenty.
And then, there you are again:
the crowing in the yard,
the dancing around,
the pecking and scratching,
the sudden rush,
the outstretched wings,
the ecstatic death-
defying rise, the old urge
tearing away at the insides,
the thrusting, the lunging,
the terrible impulse that survives
whoever wins, while the hens
nestle quietly in their straw-
filled wooden boxes,
all round and soft and eggy,
totally unconcerned
about the infernal
ruckus outside.

Three for Norman Borlaug

I The Development of the Mexican Dwarf Wheat Plant

A short plant has less stalk.
The less stalk, the more grain;
the more protein in the grain,
the less will bend and clog
the combine or fall over.

When access to the sun
is equal and ready,
there is no need
to fight for it,
to waste one's energy
trying to grow taller
than one's neighbor.
When everyone's fed,
there is more to eat.
When there is more to eat,
stronger arms carry the load and share it.
This is a new, man-made development.
It did not happen naturally.
Think about that.

II On The Relationship Between Food and Peace

You cannot carry peace
on shoulders that are weak,
with bones that are bent
or a stomach that is crying.

****

You cannot
shake a hand
with a hand
you cannot lift,
although you can
make a fist.

****

What you don't feed
will never grow,
will never love,
will never be strong enough
to hold or save you.

****

Peace comes
when it's least
expected, when
the dishes are done
and you stare
from the sink
out the window
toward the horses grazing
in the blooming meadow.

III Today

Each morning
the future comes
sneaking its red head
up over the horizon.
Your neck shivers
when your eyes see it.
And what does it bring,
in time, but the present,
the same cup of coffee
in the same trembling hands.

In the end, you have
what you've always had,
your heart, your brain,
a crumbling body,
who knows how many
second chances.

Every sunrise
calls out to you, the birds call,
the crops, the flowers, the cats,
the dog, the cattle, the chickens,
your loving wife and family,
all the huddled starving masses
so far away --
and you do what you can
to answer.

11

out-of-the-body travel

the δreacɦ of ɭife

How many living things
live in your house with you?
Have you ever thought about it?
Oh, you've seen the stray moth
in the flour or the worm in the basement drain,
I'm sure, and thought nothing of it.
The line of ants stretching across the kitchen counter
up the south wall all the way across
the back side of the house to God knows where else.
And don't forget the squirrel that gets in
each winter and runs across the piano keys and
chews the windowpanes, and the mice in the attic
and the ancient nest-filled walls,
and the mosquitoes, and the beetles,
and the crickets, and the termites
and the rats the dogs are always chasing,
and the opossum in the dryer,
and the cats and the fish.
How could you forget the fish?
You don't have a bird anymore do you?
So we can strike that one off the list!
Except for the red-headed woodpecker
pecking on the shutters,
and the blue jay and the cardinal
at the feeder, and the humming bird
over by the flowers, and the owl overhead,
and the hawk watching everything from the tree.
How about the frog under the wooden
platform in the basement shower
and the sly snake hiding over in the damp shadows?
How about your spouse and your children?
We mustn't forget them! Mustn't we?
And your heart. It's alive isn't it
and every cell in your body? Funny
how they all know exactly how you are feeling,
simultaneously, instantaneously, even before you do.
It's hard to avoid the conclusion that, they too, are thinking.

And what about all your hair cells, and your flesh cells,
and blood cells always fighting off nasty invaders?
(Well, most of them anyway.)
How about all those bad bacteria and viruses,
and all the microbes and enzymes in your stomach and
your large and small intestines putting in their overtime
without your even knowing about it? How about every organ in your body?
I have heard men in white say that, from a purely scientific point of view,
you are proportionally as empty as the cosmic void,
that the electrons and the nucleus in every atom in your body
are spinning in exact proportion to the matter and emptiness in the cosmos.
That you are as infinite inwardly as the sky is outwardly.
My God, I wonder if there is any intelligent life in there!
How many Earths fall each morning when you brush your hair,
how many minute galaxies?
Are you really made of the same stuff
that is spinning in the heavens?
Are the heavens really made of you?
As above, you know, so below.
As above, so below.
I wonder who really lives in your house with you?
And I don't just mean those four walls made of wood.
Don't get territorial! Think of these words as a kind of knocking.
Knock, Knock. Knock. – Knock. Knock. Knock.
Is there anybody home? Are you listening?
Is this home for any body? For everybody?
God, it's a wonder you can even hear me
with the whole universe breathing.

transubstantiation

When I look
in your direction,
don't think
I am seeing you
exactly. I am
seeing skin
particles,
bone, marrow,
the inscrutable
scrambled egg
of a brain
making its billions
of minute calculations.
I see electrons
circling nuclei.
I see things
so tiny and
so vast that
I begin to
disappear entirely.
Here I go
again. Hello?
Hello! Goodbye
my confused
but happy dears.
I too am not
whom you see
before you;
I am the flame
around your head,
a thought
in your hands,
the many
trembling pages
you are holding
and trying so nobly
to make sense of.

on the way to the inevitable

The door you stand before,
you have stood before before
and never known it,
never seen its tall
gleaming panels,
its firm rich wood,
the outlandish hinges.
It has been there
secretly all your life,
as you slipped
your small growing body
over threshold
after threshold
knowing only
that something opened
when you smelled
the fresh air
on the other side.
Now you turn
the cold porcelain knob,
white as bone, and wonder
where is it you are going
(if going it can be called),
which way is in
and which out,
knowing that soon
you will hear
a click and feel
the latch give way
and at last you
will be alone
with whatever
has been waiting,
for ages it seems,
for you to enter.

the blind leading the blind

My collie reads
Plato in the dimly-
lit living room
while the children
watch TV.

She doesn't mind
that she is color blind.
The meaning of the words
sprout rainbows.

My white lab sits
on my stomach
like when he was a puppy
and licks the whiskers
clean off my tired chin.
I tell him that he is bigger
than me now but he tells me
that I am interrupting his meditation.

And the poor neurotic beagle
"Lady" is the wrong word for her.
Neither is she a "gentleman."
She humps everything in sight.
When everyone else has gone to the mall
I sit alone with my overgrown puppies
and the no-longer kittens.
We let our souls unite.
We play chess in front of the fire
and talk in our own primitive way
about what would happen
to the world if everyone
suddenly realized
that they were beautiful.

learning to count

There is one finger
then a space
with an infinite number of theoretical points,
a space so long and so deep
that you could never get
even halfway across it,
or a quarter way, or an eighth or even a sixteenth.
Then, of course, there is
the second finger
and another infinite number of points
in a tiny endless cosmos of nothingness.

To get even to two
has taken me a million years,
a billion. Who remembers for sure?
First I was a star, then a rock,
then a mountain. It was so far back now
that I became this flower.
I can't remember.
Who has even
gotten started, really?
Who has the time
in one puny life
or even knows how
to count their sorrows
or their blessings?

to the begrudgers

Okay, enough pretense.
I'm doing it now.
I'm doing it for you
so you won't have
to strain yourself.
It was labor enough
to sink the post hole
and drop in the telephone pole.
My God, it was big,
but I sang while doing it.
I even whistled!
Did you recognize the song?
Of course you didn't,
your heart was already
beating to the tune
your head was singing
as I hauled up the crosspiece.

To nail the left hand
and my feet was no big
problem, but to nail the right
by myself, now that *would* be a miracle.
One I don't feel up to right now.

You've got to admit. So far
this is the performance of my life.
That must be why you are clapping and
nodding toward each other. That must be why you smile.
Thank you, dear friends, dear countrymen,
dear profferers of the crown.
I wave to you as you strip my clothing.
I shake your hand as you dip the sponge
and pierce my bloated heart.
I will gladly exit this world for you.
I will gladly ascend,
but you will have to do *something*.
You will have to talk to me as I go.

Pray to me. Pray for me.
Tell me you are sorry I am leaving.
Ask me how long I'll be gone.

meditation

I can't get
much smaller
than I am
already. No one
else can even
see me. Still,
I'm too big
I suppose, for
happiness.

I am the stone
in the stream
my life
washes over.
I am the
bloody soiled
bandages
on the
invisible man.

I can't be
much quieter
than this whisper
I am making,
this thin scribbling
on the void.
How you have
even come
to hear it
is a mystery.

If I could be
and not be,
then maybe
something pure
and loving and holy
would flood in

the emptiness
I've prepared.

But there is
no such thing
as silence.
Even when
I still myself
and make
no sound,
something
deafening
rushes around.
Inside, always
this fear
of conclusions,
this drum.
Always, this same
terrible beating.

the keening

I had just
emptied the bin
and set up
the auger
in order to
fill it --
autumn and
night
falling forever.

Soon it was
too dark
to work.
That's when
the dogs
pricked their ears
and barked
as if a storm
were coming.

The sky was clear.
I didn't hear
a thing at first.
Then it settled
upon me, like
an old thought
suddenly remembered --
a wailing, a woman,
out of control
helplessly, hopelessly
wailing.

It couldn't
have been.
There wasn't
a house around
for miles -- nothing

but coyotes sleeping
in the banks of the creek.
Still it echoed
off the hills
and the house;
it echoed
deep inside me.

The kittens
stopped playing.
Their mother
looked up
from her cleaning
and listened intently
as if to hear
in whose direction,
this time,
the sky was about
to fall.

archaeology

She was buried
with a lone needle
in her slender hands
and he with a spear beside him.
An elaborate shield
laid upon his chest
as if there was something to fight
where he was headed,
as if the wheels of his chariot
had not come unhinged
aeons ago. All these years
she's been looking at the sky
as she did so often in life,
staring at all those bright
tears in the heavenly fabric.
How far away they seem,
how cold a burning.
It's been thousands of years,
so many lifetimes, and now
the sudden indignity of our poking.
Still her face remains undisturbed,
fine, emotionless -- watching.

darkness

Night comes on,
encircles, then
draws near.
It crawls
inside the little
holes in your
window screen,
spreads itself out
across the bed
where it grows
and grows
and covers you
until you are
inside it.

Then it takes
you where
you never
thought to go
and lets you
hear what
will never
be said.
Then, it touches
your eyes
softly and
your limbs
and you can't move,
can't breathe,
can't smile
and you wonder,
(although
you think
you know)
if you're alive
or if
you're dreaming.

walking across lake okoboji

It would be easier
if I said that it is winter,
January in fact,
26 below and fat
fishermen in bulky overalls
are squatting here and there
in their heated wooden huts.

But it isn't. Imagine that,
when we walk off the dock
and stride toward Gull Point in the west.
The sea gulls tilting their astonished heads
as bass, pike and bluegill
follow our underwater shadows.
The bottoms of our bare feet
emerge and disappear
from the surface of
their rippling sky.
As always, water laps
against our ankles, but this time
there is no rock to cut
or bang or bruise them.
Imagine we are smoke
spreading across the summer sky
like the late cries
of hidden children
disappearing in the fall.

still wandering, aengus

Alone, in the wilderness
one is never alone.
There is always
that bright stranger
just up ahead
on the other side
of the bushes
or the trees
or the wildflowers
beckoning you onward.
And when you follow
she is gone, always.
And you are left
standing alone
but not alone
with the infinitely
various foliage
and that ghost-hand,
that mysterious,
nearly-invisible shining
that never tires
of its many invitations.

at the monastery

in memory of Brother Gus, for the brothers of New Melleray Abbey, Peosta Iowa

The monks have been
sitting in silence
so long that
when they speak,
they speak hardly
in a whisper.

You have to
lean forward
and bend
your back
just to hear
them. When
they move,
they move slowly.
Yesterday
I asked
Brother August
for a book
from his library.
Tomorrow
he will have
it off the shelf.
The day after
he will turn
and give it to me.
"You can read it,"
he said, only if the
words passing
through your eyes
make no sound.
You may
turn the pages
only if the air
becomes more

still
because of
your turning.

dialogue between self and soul

One day
I opened my mouth
and a bird flew out,
a pretty bird,
like one
I had never
seen before
at the feeder.

It called
to me, but
I could not
decipher
its singing.

Still every
time I spotted it,
every time I
climbed the
golden ladder
of its notes,
my body
grew lighter
and tinier.

Soon we will be
the same small size;
soon we will both
be bright and beautiful
and no one
will be able
to distinguish us
from our songs.

First communion

Oh, the moment
my soul was cleansed and
I mouthed my prayers,
the moment I folded
my sad hands
in front of my white jacket
and white shirt and tie,
my white pants and socks
and shoes, from that moment,
I began looking for you:
in my room,
under the bed, behind the dressers,
in books, in school,
in the words of others,
in the hearts of long-dead men.
I prayed and prayed
that you would come.
I started looking, Lord,
hard everywhere
for some sure little sign
in this strange world,
looking, looking, looking,
not knowing,
thinking, dreaming
that I was blind
from birth.

in defense of darkness

Soybeans pod
when the sky
is right. It has
nothing to do
with age, or size
or readiness.
It has to do
with darkness and day.
Whatever height
the plants are at
when heaven provides
the right proportion,
they bring forth
all they can
in the condition
they're in.
Something in the
heart of night
triggers them --
silence, sleep, sorrow.
It's as simple as that.
You could fill
their evenings with
brilliant suns.
You could pray and dance,
but it would accomplish nothing.
It's not the day,
it's the night,
that makes all the difference.

III

a place at the table

monarchs and mowing in september

Once again,
I state the obvious
with the proviso
"I am not
making this up."
but today, every-
where I've ridden,
on whatever tractor,
butterflies have followed
risen and dived around me.
Mowing the weeds
along the fence line,
on the borders
of the farms,
on the road,
under the
front yard cedars --
hundreds,
thousands,
hundreds of thousands,
who knows,
the bare arms
of the Chinese elms
were orange
with wings,
with leaves
fluttering
to the ground
and then back
up again,
floating around
my heavy body,
trying to tell
me something.
I have never
experienced
anything like their

generosity and number,
such a quiet beauty,
so insistent,
so here, so
suddenly here
knocking me
in the head,
waving before my eyes,
a beauty until now
I could only
believe was possible,
bred in a faraway country,
in a field
no one has seen,
in a dream,
in a dream
it takes hope
and love
and two tiny eyes to find
and a minuscule brain
and the most delicate wings.

saying goodbye to poetry

Halfway to Topeka I realized
I left my poems
on the roof of the car.
Not just a "sheaf" but
five years worth of
who knows how much
of my much-examined,
disconsolate life?

I drove back and forth
for hours but by then
my words were
planting themselves
in the richest farmland on earth.

I wonder what will
grow from them
in the spring ahead.
When the rains fall
and the sun comes
I will drive out
over the horizon.
I will slow my car
to a crawl
and watch
for something new
and unspeakable
taking root and
glittering in the weeds.

TWISTER

In a dream
my late father came to me.
He was rumpled and grumpy
but secretly kind as always.
But before he could
open his mouth,
he stepped into a hole
beside my bed
and fell through the floor.
His gruff Brooklyn voice
trailed behind him
down the windy vortex.
I could hear my late Midwestern
mother calling up to me,
she waved and smiled
as she spun round
and around and around
with my late aunts and uncles
and my late grandparents.
They were all speaking
at once and their words
kept getting smaller.
I knelt down to listen.
I quieted everything,
even my brain, even my heart.
But I could make out
nothing useful.
When I bent over
the edge of my covers
I almost fell in myself.
To tell the truth,
I almost had a mind to.
I wondered what it would be like
splashing around in that dark
well of echoes.

the man who is allergic to laughter

Maybe it all started
when he was young
and some fungus
from a bin full
of rotting beans
made his lungs
sensitive to
strong emotion.
Maybe he thought
about himself too much
when he first heard
that God was dying
and the universe
spreading itself thin.
Maybe he's just afraid
to enjoy things
for fear he will
be asked to leave them.
It's ridiculous now,
to ponder. "It's inside,"
he says, "The problem
is inside my body."
All he knows is the tickle
in his chest
and the spasms
one faint smile
will set in motion.
When his children
run to him sweetly
or, Heaven forbid,
tell him a joke,
his body bends
in convulsions.
He slaps his thighs
and folds forward
in what seems
the grandest

of guffaws.
No one sees
the pain he's in;
no one thinks
he's suffering.
When people see
tears squeezed
from the corners
of his eyes,
they are grateful,
happy even, because
they know something
has set him to laughing.

бiяd caτcheя

for Ron Harms

It is not for food
that I come to the hills
and stake the dirt with poles.
It is just to feel the soft feathers
in my trembling hands,
to touch them with numbers
and free them from the nets
I have spent all morning
concocting. Each song
is precious to me now.
No words can describe
what wells up inside,
not these or any other,
when I listen to the
bright, frightened bodies
curve around my limbs
and then fall up into the blue
on the other side of the underbrush.

There is only half the number
there was when I first started.
Half the eyes.
Half the wings.
Half the music
over half the farms
over half the soil
and half the farmers.
In the past ten years
half the world I knew
and am and came from
has vanished.
I come each day to name
what is
no longer here.

iowa landscape -- september 1994

for David and Pamela Clinefelter

How many swelling hills
have I sailed over,
how much
endless sky?
Everywhere I turn
it's the same story
spoken differently:
each blade of grass,
each fledgling weed,
each sprouting tree
burning green,
burning white
in the black soil;
the sun's vast expanse
falling softly
through each leaf;
our one short life
covered, again
and again,
by the infinite frost,
by the minute
glittering dew,
by silence,
by whatever
is open and ready
and rooted,
near and afar,
by whatever is
reaching out of itself
and growing
the whole green world round?

the hawk in the grasswas

The hawk's beautiful feathers
were still attached to their quills,
still embedded in bone
almost hidden in the grass.
By then, there was no
crown or beak, no coldly
ferocious eyes, no gnawing belly
keeping them searching,
just two groups of curved talons
and outstretched wings
hovering now on a different wind
coming up over the horizon.

the unbidden

While driving to the county courthouse,
it came over him.
He hardly felt it at first.
His fist gripped the steering wheel.
Then he ran his fingers
over the dashboard of his truck
as if it were the forehead of a feverish lover.
By the time he got where he was going,
he didn't want to be where he was.
Wave after wave washed over him,
then settled in his throat, the saltiest water.
He wanted to crawl out of his skin and
go to the other side of the auditor's office.
He wanted to see himself as others saw him:
calm, patient, straight-backed in line,
a solid man paying his bills.
He wanted to look around the room
and smile at his neighbors
and believe again, in the
comforting texture of surfaces.

Local history

for the Fremont County Historical Society

Who knows
what they wanted,
if they found
what they
were looking for
when they came
and settled
or left or simply
looked around
and passed through?

What do we know
of them really,
but the soil
they stood on
for the briefest
of moments,
and the snow
and the rain
and the sun,
the ever oppressive sun,
though even all that
is changed
and changing?

What we know
of them
is what we
know of ourselves.
There is no such thing
as a fact, really.
History is not
what *happened*.
It is what someone
said happened

and what someone
and someone repeated
after that. It is
what lives inside.
Things are
and then they are not.
All there is then,
is words --
in the beginning,
in the end --
every sacred
consonant and vowel
of them, words,
words, these words
echoing through
our myriad heads.

prayer to the holy ground

in memory of Ralph Costello

Dear earth,
dear dirt,
dear fluff of ancient decay,
hold me today
as you have
without my
even knowing.

Wherever I have gone,
whoever I have been,
I have never left
your outstretched arms.
Whatever I am in,
you are
under it;
you are behind
whatever man or woman
has come to design
in the feverish mind.

Forgive us,
please,
our arrogance,
our innocence,
our ignorance
of your
terrible power,
of your vast,
unthinkable love;
hold us all
a little
while longer;
teach us
to look into
your dark eyes

and to listen
and to praise,
praise, praise
before we fall into them
and come out again
transformed,
into something
even more
unimaginably beautiful.

playing opossum

When the opossum
senses danger
he does not *play*,
he *dies* or
comes as close
to death
as he can
this side
of Heaven.
His small
simple brain
overloads,
then his whole body
gives in
and falls
disconnected
from fear,
from its very self,
from every
howling dog
that is circling.

And when he wakes
(if he wakes)
a short while later,
no one around
is sniffing.
There is only
the bright world
he steps into
suddenly, briskly, blindly,
without even memory
to guide him.

the pain of this world

for Cailín

See our collie
come prancing now
from the coop,
her soft thin snout
quivering with
the limp body
of a dead mink.
See her lay it
by another
in the clipped
front-yard grass.

She is proud,
so proud.

She does not think
its red fur *beautiful*.
She is not ashamed
of the blood
on her paws.
She looks up
from her most recent display
of secret carnage
with the mildest
of love
in her eyes.

in season

My wife sips her coffee
and reads the paper
while I melt into the couch,
immersed in some new poet's
spiritual Odyssey.
Two fields away,
on the upper lip
of the second terrace,
two black objects
move silently
across the winter hills.
My wife sees them
and bears witness.
I cannot, at first,
make out what she is
talking about and then,
there they are. Through
the dark branches
of our backyard
I can see farther and farther
toward the horizon.
Suddenly, I know
just where to look,
and catch a quick glimpse
of other branches moving
toward us — a doe and a stag
mirroring our quiet morning,
a husband and a wife
intent, listening,
picking their tentative way
over this season's
bright and unyielding
crust of snow.

the wonder of photosynthesis

in memory of Sylvan Runkel

First, there is light --
a distant, warm vibration.
Then, there is food
becoming food
becoming food,
then there is you
many green
aeons later,
standing in your clothes,
so much food
full of food,
hungry yourself,
and looking around,
wondering
where on earth
you came from.

the first calendar

The Mayans, it is said,
discovered zero
300 years after the
death of Christ
but they didn't tell
anyone. India didn't
even get wind of it
until 600.

I wonder where
it was hiding?
How they could tell
they had it.
"Come here!
Look at this!
Nothing in my hands!"
It's no wonder
no one believed them.
Without it, it is said,
no one could hold
a place value.
Without zero
there are no tens
or 100's or 1000's.
How could there be?
Nothing from nothing
is nothing.
Nothing times anything
in the world is nothing.
Add nothing to
whatever you have
and you have
what you had before.
This is the secret
they kept hidden
down in old Mexico
away from all those

yet to be born
noisy Americans
who believe
that more is better,
that there is never enough,
that silence is precious
only once it's broken.
"See there, kids,
behind that bush --
nothing. Hear there,
in your heart, that silence,
time outside of time,
feel once and for all
the vast round emptiness,
the eyeless, nose-less,
chicken-less egg
that gave birth
to millennia."

song of the modern luddite

for Myron Marty

The TV was
the first to go,
then the radio.
I smiled as
I watched them
sailing through
the open window
mouthing their
urgent nonsense
at the stars.

It felt good
to be suddenly
liberated,
so good
I decided
to pull the plug
on everything
I owned
that owned me,
to find all the time
that was saved
and to give it back
to the trees
and the birds
and the dirt.

No more
angry heads
ranting their bile
in my home.
No more
Homer and Marge.
Even the President
now just mouths

his speeches soundlessly.
No more dead eyes
watching other lives
living my life for me.
No headlines,
no cable,
no monthly bills
to stay alive.
"O, shut it off,"
I said,
"tune it out
one moment,
one day,
one life
at a time."

No need to know
which is the dream
and which
the reality,
which moment
is the moment
that will last.
It is enough
to hear
and to remember
for a time,
anytime one can,
that no news
is good news
and that silence,
ah silence,
is still
the sweetest
music
in the world.

First Lesson in Tracking

for Jean Braley

If you're good,
you don't need to see
what it is you're tracking.
The space it has gone to
has emptied the space
it has been, leaving messages.
A good birder doesn't
look for spectacular
red and yellow feathers
screeching in the green branches.
Anyone can do that.
She just knows *to* look
and *where*, how to *be*
what she is following.

What we have, first of all,
is not the fox or the raccoon
or the squirrel or the
acorn he was hoarding,
not the thin bristle
around its rim,
not even the oak
she was nesting in.
What we have mostly
is what we believe in,
something glinting in the tall grasses
at the edge of our field of vision.
There is evidence, believe me,
if you have a mind to find it.
There is evidence, always,
when you look closely,
that everything you thought you owned,
that everything you thought you knew,
you didn't.

the ROCKS in the fields around us

The rocks
in the fields
around us
move
even though
we think
they do not.
They break.
They change.
They remember
the heat
of the fire.

Ask them
your most
burning questions;
trust them
with your soft life.
They will answer you.
They will share
their stories
with any listener
patient enough
to wait
more
than a lifetime.

a place at the table

I can taste the sun
in the peaches
of the orchard.
I can taste the wind
in your hair,
your soft skin
furry with
its pale down.

There is a sweetness
in the space between
the things we
come from
and go to,
inside whatever
we touch.
More and more
I feel it, waiting,
whenever I open the door.
I say, "Thank you."
even in the darkness.
I say, "Thank you."
for a place
at this inexhaustible table
to which we all
have come,
sometimes the guest,
sometimes the dinner.
I say, "Thank you.
Thank you.
Thank you. Thank You."
Each day,
I savor
the sweetness.

to a blooming blackberry

Berries bloom
all by themselves,
all by themselves,
for no reason.
Wine ripens
in each leaf,
for no reason,
all by itself.
You can weed
and feed and prune
and it matters little.
In this land
of scattered voices,
in this time
of coming night,
each small vine
still remembers
to turn itself
toward the light.

on hearing voices

This morning
you wake late
and say nothing.

For the rest of the day
you sit in silence
in a chair
and read, maybe,
or think
(because your mind must)
about nothing.

Hours pass,
and those
around you
begin to
ask questions.

They ask you to move.
They ask you to do
what the TV has told them.
But you are already
the surface of the pond
at which you are staring,
and they already
are a faint jumble
of fading voices.

Only then
do the wrens sing
and spring's buds
bloom around you.

One by one,
clouds float
over the fields
you have planted,

dark and heavy
with blessings.

You know, now, suddenly,
when the wind comes,
the wind comes.
It speaks louder
than anything.

song of burdens

A squirrel jumps
and a branch bends
with its landing
then rises after
it goes, twice
the height
it was before.
Something about
its sudden burden
has lifted it,
the squirrel
itself maybe
has strung it
to its small
animal body
pulling its
bent back
up where it
longs to be,
straighter, higher,
lighter
with the weight
of where
it has been.

the fine line between a nap and poetry

How sweetly
the eyes surrender,
the jaw goes slack,
the head falls back,
falls, every bone
in the body falls
where it sits
while the brain
goes on thinking.
The pen in your hand
will do you
no good now,
no magic wand
could pull you
from the stupor
that has suddenly
washed over.
Ah but, little
by little, words
too, fall
into place.
A smile forms
on your face
mysteriously,
your hands drop
from behind
your head.
Soon, you are
beyond yourself
and something other
moves in,
begins forming
inside you:
a song maybe,
a prayer, an answer,
a feeling, instruction,
a thought, years from now,

everyone else
will be thinking...
every changed
unsuspecting one
who, even now, imagines
you are dreaming.

posing for my brother in portland, oregon

On the broken sidewalk
by the old warehouses,
elevators, mills, trains
and railroad tracks
Owen walks the streets,
tripod upon his shoulder,
like a smiling hobo.
A construction worker
whistles and waves
and points at himself
from atop a steamroller.
He has seen my brother
many times on this
same corner,
with movie stars and models,
by these same
man hole covers
stacked and ready
for sewers. He wants
Owen to make his life,
too, seem beautiful,
to take the dirty sleeveless tee
from off his back,
the cigarette stains
from his teeth,
to somehow make
a beer belly look sexy.
I know how he feels,
but Owen has enough
on his hands right now,
no professional this time,
no nude, God forbid,
nothing anyone would
want to see more of
or more closely
or allow the young
to witness *in toto*

unless it was
a form of punishment.

Maybe he'll focus
on a pore and let
the rest of me go hazy.
Sometimes the background
is more important
than a smile,
something I can't offer
today without a reason
and, to me, nothing in
this industrial underbelly
is singing.

Oh, I know
there's nothing
a photographer can do
to make you younger,
leaner, less gray,
although a good one
might make you
appear that way,
for one one hundredth
of a second, for one
one hundredth of a second
he might trick the sun
into the wrinkles on your skin
so that what is underneath
floods in, so that the way it is
is the way it ought to be,
maybe for a second,
for one one hundredth
of a second but
that's long enough,
believe me,
plenty long enough,
to see it,
to change your image,

to feel it,
to freeze it forever,
to burn, to burn
a little paper with light.

Acknowledgement is made to the following magazines in which the following poems first appeared:

The Briar Cliff Review: "Playing Opossum"
Christian Century: "To a Blooming Blackberry," "First Communion"
Contemporary Review: "Prayer to the Holy Ground," "Once When the Ground Was Holy," "The Wind in my Bedroom Window"
Defined Providence: "The Man Who is Allergic to Laughter," "Posing for my Brother in Portland, Oregon"
The Laurel Review: "Lowland," "Sleepwalking"
New Letters: "The Blind Leading the Blind," "Learning to Count," "To the Begrudgers"
Sycamore Roots: "Bird Catcher," "The Wonder of Photosynthesis," "First Lesson in Tracking"
Trapeze: "The Arrogance of Staying Put," "A Place at the Table," "On Hearing Voices," "Setting Traps"

The author would like to express his gratitude to the following who commissioned him to write certain poems:

Jon Chenette of Grinnell College for his choral work *Broken Ground* commissioned by the Des Moines Symphony Orchestra, The Iowa Sesquicentennial Commission, and Grinnell College in honor of the sesquicentennials in 1996 of the state of Iowa and Grinnell College. First performed at the Des Moines Civic Center on May 11&12, 1996 by the Grinnell College Singers directed by John Stuher-Rommereim and the Des Moines Symphony Orchestra conducted by Joseph Giunta: "Once When the Ground was Holy," "Iowa Landscape – September 1994"

The Fremont County Historical Society, Sidney, Iowa for its 1996 Iowa sesquicentennial compilation of local history: "Local History"

The World Food Prize Foundation and the Norman Borlaug Heritage Foundation for the October 18, 2001 celebration at the Des Moines Civic Center of the 100th anniversary of the Nobel Peace Prize, the 31st anniversary of Norman Borlaug's winning of the Nobel Peace Prize, and the 15th anniversary of his establishment of the World Food Prize: "The Development of the Mexican Dwarf Wheat Plant," "On the Relationship between Food and Peace," "Today"

The Loess Hills Prairie Seminar: "Bird Catcher," "The Wonder of Photosynthesis"

The 1994 Iowa State Conference of the United Church of Christ held at Grinnell College: "The Wind in my Bedroom Window," "On Hearing Voices," "A Place at the Table," "To a Blooming Blackberry"

"The Holy Ground," "Monarchs and Mowing in September" and "Iowa Landscape – September 1994" were first published in the anthology *Voices on the Landscape: Contemporary Iowa Poets*, Loess Hills Books, Farragut, Iowa 1996

The author would like to especially thank James McKean and Robert Schultz for their invaluable criticism and support.

photo by Owen Carey

Michael Carey lives and farms in southwest Iowa with his wife Kelly and their four children: Helen, Maeve, Andrew and Fionnuala. His work has been widely published in literary magazines across the United States, Great Britain and Ireland. He and his work have been featured in *The Wall Street Journal*, *Time*, *The Associated Press*, *World Monitor Today*, *The Des Moines Register*, *Read*, *Country America*, *Successful Farmer*, *Iowa Farmer Today* and Iowa Public Television's *Studio III Presents*, *Touchstone* and *Take One* programs.

In 1997 Mr. Carey received the Iowa Council of Teachers of English *Friend of Literacy Award* for his work with young writers in the schools.

In 2001 he founded and hosts *Voices from the Prairie* a weekly radio program sponsored by Humanities Iowa, KUNI Public Radio of Cedar Falls, and KMA Broadcasting of Shenandoah featuring Iowa poetry. The show is syndicated to radio stations all across Iowa.

Most summers he teaches at the University of Iowa's *Summer Writing Festival*.